FESTIVALS AND CELEBRATIONS

Kathleen Elliott

YOUNG LIBRARY

Contents

First published in 1984 by
Young Library Limited
International Press Centre
76 Shoe Lane, London EC4A 3JB
Second impression 1985

ISBN 0 946003 24 6

Printed and bound by
Robert Hartnoll Ltd
Bodmin, Cornwall

Designed by Fred Price

Throughout this book, references to dates are all of the Gregorian calendar unless otherwise stated.

Introduction

Everyone enjoys a celebration. People have been holding festivals ever since they have had anything to be thankful for. Ancient civilizations celebrated the coming of spring after the cold days of winter. Farming peoples held festivals to thank the gods for a successful harvest.

Some religious festivals are very ancient. Many of the Jewish and Hindu festivals that you will read about in this book were first celebrated thousands of years ago. Many Christian saints' days are also very

old. Other religious festivals are more recent in origin.

There are also festivals which celebrate historical events like victory in battle, or the birthdays of great people. In the last 200 years or so (and especially in the last 40 years) many countries have won independence from colonial masters, and celebrate independence days.

There are also festivals which are held nowadays simply for fun, or to celebrate the end of a sombre period like Lent or Ramadan.

Nowadays, most countries (especially those to which many peoples have emigrated recently – Britain, the USA, Australia, New Zealand and South Africa) have a mixture of races and religions. So, within these countries, a great variety of festivals are celebrated every year.

You will discover all kinds of festivals in this book. You might even like to try celebrating some which are new to you! There are lots of tips on how to do it, and I hope this book helps to make your life just a little bit jollier.

6

1
Calendar Festivals

In this chapter you will read about festivals which celebrate things that happen at a particular time of the year. Although they are now calendar or seasonal festivals they were originally linked with religious ceremonies. However, in many cases, the religious significance of the occasion is today largely forgotten or ignored.

New Year

New Year is a time to turn your back on the old, and look forward to the new. In the Gregorian calendar, which is used by Christian countries and most other countries, New Year's Day falls on 1st January. (1st January has not always been New Year's Day, and even today many religious communities celebrate their new year at other times – see pages 8, 39, 45, and 51).

New Year's Eve is a time for holding parties. They usually go on until after midnight, which is the moment the new year begins. In Britain, Europe, and other countries where Europeans have settled, the custom of first-footing is practised. The first male visitor to a house after midnight

The Cape Colored community in South Africa take over the football stadiums to celebrate Second New Year's Day in riotous fashion.

on 1st January is supposed to bring good luck. (Female visitors are believed to be unlucky!) Usually the visitor brings a gift, such as money, bread, or coal, which is supposed to ensure that the family will have plenty of such things during the year to come.

In the U.S.A., 1st January is a day for parades. The most famous is the Tournament of the Roses Parade, held at Pasadena, California. Flower-decked carriages fill the streets, and the Rose Bowl football game is played to the delight of thousands.

Meanwhile in South Africa, where 1st January falls in midsummer, church bells and gunshots combine to welcome the new year. For the coloured community of Cape Province, New Year's Day and 'Second New Year's Day' (2nd January), are carnival days, when people dress in colourful costumes, and dance in the streets and in soccer stadiums to the sound of riotous music.

Chinese New Year

Chinese New Year may begin at any time between 21st January and 19th February. It begins with the first new moon during that period, and lasts for two weeks. The festival is celebrated in many countries around the world where there are large Chinese communities.

Chinese New Year begins as a family celebration – a time for visiting friends and relatives, settling old debts, and buying new clothes. The celebrations end with a three-day lantern festival. Homes display

A Chinese lantern

At New Year, Chinese people love to decorate their homes and temples with lanterns. To make a lantern for your house or classroom, all you need is a rectangular piece of paper. Paint it a bright colour.

Fold it in half lengthwise and then make cuts as shown in the diagram, ending about 2 or 3 cm (1 inch) from the open edge.

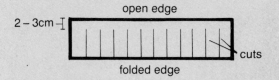

When you open out the paper it should look like this:

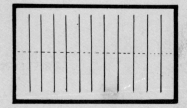

Roll the paper round to make a cylinder and glue the edges together. Flatten the shape slightly and attach a strip of paper to the top to make a handle. Your lantern should look like this:

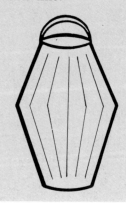

lanterns to symbolize the lengthening of the days and their increasing warmth.

The most famous and flamboyant of these processions takes place in the Chinese quarter of San Francisco in the U.S.A. There is a huge, noisy parade with colourful floats, and marching units

Vast crowds fill San Francisco's streets to enjoy the Chinese New Year.

dressed in beautiful costumes. Star of the parade is the 125-foot long golden dragon, which is hand-made of Chinese silk and velvet. The dragon has the head of a camel, the horns of a deer, the neck of a snake, the claws of a hawk, the belly of a frog, and the scales of a fish. It weaves its way through the streets to the music of gongs, cymbals, drums, and firecrackers.

A similar parade takes place in Soho in

9

A colourful dragon prances through Soho in London's Chinese New Year parade.

London, although the dragon this time looks rather more like a lion. The houses of the Chinese people, and their temples, are decorated with flags and lanterns.

May Day

The first day of May was a spring festival in Europe for many centuries. The custom nearly died out later but, happily, in this century there has been a May Day revival.

In Britain and the United States children make May baskets from paper. These are filled with flowers and hung on friends' doors. The prettiest girl of the district is chosen as May Queen. There is fun, music, song, and dancing around the maypole. In the United States, May Day is the day when girls' schools and colleges hold their May dances.

Labour Day

1st May is also Labour Day in many countries. This is a festival dedicated to labouring people. There are marches, bands, and speeches by socialist politicians and trade union leaders. In the U.S.S.R.

Massed ranks of soldiers march through the streets during a May Day parade in the Soviet Union.

there is always a big military parade in Moscow or Leningrad.

In the United States, and in some provinces of Canada, Labour Day is celebrated on the first Monday in September.

Partly to counteract the socialist Labour Day, many states in the U.S.A hold a 'Loyalty Day'. There are parades of boy scouts, veterans of the armed forces, and drum and bugle corps.

Harvest

Harvest festivals have been celebrated for almost as long as people have been growing plants for food. They are held to give

Dancers celebrate at the Barossa Valley wine festival in South Australia.

thanks to God for a successful harvest. The modern Christian Harvest Festival originated with Lammas ('Loaf Mass'), held every year on 1st August. Bread baked from the first sheaf of the harvest was brought to the church to be blessed.

Nowadays, harvest festivals can be either religious or non-religious. In Europe, harvest thanksgiving is held around the end of September. Corn, vegetables, and fruits

The fruits of the earth are displayed in churches during the harvest thanksgiving festival.

are brought to church and displayed at the altar, and special services are held. Later the foods are given to the old and needy.

In countries of the southern hemisphere, harvest season falls in various months between January and April. The wheat harvest festivals fall in January. The apple harvest in Tasmania is celebrated in March, and the grape harvest from the Barossa Valley in South Australia is celebrated in April.

2
Historical Festivals

People will celebrate all sorts of historical events. These may include the day their country was discovered by Europeans, or the day it became independent and self-governing. Great victories in battle, or the end of a long war, are also celebrated. Celebrations are not always happy, for example many countries set aside a day to honour men who gave their lives fighting for the country. There are also celebrations of events which were not very important but which have caught the public imagination, and provide an opportunity for light-hearted enjoyment.

For over 140 years New Zealand's Maoris have celebrated Waitangi Day.

Waitangi Day

This New Zealand holiday commemorates the day on 6th February 1840 when 512 Maori chiefs signed the Treaty of Waitangi with the British government. This treaty gave complete control of the country to Britain, with the consent of the Maori chiefs. In exchange the chiefs and their tribes retained the right to own their lands, and received all the rights and privileges of British subjects.

Waitangi Day is a big day for New Zealanders because it marks the birth of the modern nation. It became the National Day of New Zealand in 1959, and a public holiday in 1973.

14

On 6th February each year a ceremony is held in the grounds of Treaty House at Waitangi. It is attended by the governor-general of New Zealand, the prime minister, and the minister of Maori Affairs. The Royal New Zealand Navy traditionally plays an important part in the ceremony, and the occasion features the famous Maori welcome.

U.S. Independence Day

The Fourth of July is a festival celebrated all over America. It commemorates that day in 1776, when the Declaration of Independence was adopted by thirteen

The U.S.A.'s Declaration of Independence is read again to an appreciative crowd.

rebel American colonies. The struggle for independence from Britain had begun several years before, and was not fully achieved until 1782. However, 4th July has always been celebrated as Independence Day.

As it is mid-summer in the U.S.A., Independence Day festivities are usually held outdoors. It is a public holiday celebrated with barbecues, parties, and picnics. Flags and banners hang in the streets, and there are historical pageants and parades in towns and cities the length and breadth of the country.

Korean settlers celebrate their ancient traditions on Australia Day.

Australia Day

In Australia, 26th January is an important day because it commemorates the foundation of the first British colony in that country. After an eight-month journey from England, a party consisting mainly of convicts and soldiers established a settlement at Sydney Cove in 1788.

Australians take a holiday on the nearest Monday to Australia Day, and there are festivities all over the country. The streets of towns and cities in many states are decorated with banners and flags. Children act in short plays, and there are carnivals and sometimes air displays too.

Two of the states of Australia also set aside special days to commemorate their founding. Western Australia's Foundation Day on 4th June celebrates the state's birth in 1826–7; and on 12th March Canberra celebrates its official birth in 1913 as the capital of Australia.

A day in July is set aside for Australians to think about the original inhabitants of their country—Aboriginal Day.

Anzac Day

The word 'ANZAC' comes from the initials of the Australian and New Zealand Army Corps. On 25th April 1915, during the First World War, this combined force of Australian and New Zealand soldiers landed on the Gallipoli Peninsula in Turkey. Their attempt to capture the peninsula failed, and many gallant soldiers lost their lives.

Today, Anzac Day is a public holiday and day of remembrance in Australia and New Zealand. People gather at war memorials and hold special religious services in honour of their dead in all wars in which they have been involved.

Columbus Day

Columbus Day is an American festival held on 12th October to celebrate the 'discovery' of the New World by a European, Christopher Columbus, in 1492. This is the day on which he landed on an island in the Caribbean, which he named San Salvador.

Columbus Day was first celebrated in New York in 1792. Now a massive parade is held every year in that city, with up to 300 bands and 75,000 people marching up Fifth Avenue. San Francisco holds a festival on the nearest Sunday to 12th October. There the celebrations begin with High Mass at the Church of Saints Peter and Paul. In the afternoon there is a parade and a re-enactment of the landing at the city's Aquatic Park. Many states across the country hold activities, especially for schoolchildren, and banks and government offices close for the day.

Americans have other festivals which are dedicated to important men in their history. These include Abraham Lincoln's birthday (12th February), George Washington's birthday (22nd February) and Forefathers' Day. Forefathers' Day, which is held on 21st December, com-

memorates the first landing of the Pilgrim Fathers in 1620.

Guy Fawkes Night

On 5th November 1605, Guy Fawkes was captured while trying to blow up the Houses of Parliament in London. Guy Fawkes, and his fellow conspirators, were all Catholics and were trying to kill the Protestant King James I, and his son Prince Henry, who were both in Parliament for the state opening ceremony.

In 1606 the government decided that 5th of November should henceforth be 'a day of thanksgiving to be celebrated with

Crowds parade through the streets by torchlight on Guy Fawkes Night.

bonfires and fireworks'. Nowadays, families around Britain enjoy the event with a large bonfire in gardens and parks, on which a 'guy' (an effigy of Guy Fawkes) is burned. The guy is often carried around the streets for weeks beforehand so that children can beg for money with which to buy fireworks to be set off around the bonfire.

Thanksgiving

Thanksgiving celebrates the first harvest in America by the Pilgrim Fathers, over 350 years ago. The Pilgrim Fathers were a

Poppies stream down during the solemn Remembrance Day service.

group of Dutch and English emigrants who had fled their own countries for religious reasons. They left Plymouth in England in September 1620 and arrived in America, at a place they named Plymouth, late in December.

After a year of trial and hardship, they gathered in their first harvest the following autumn.

Thanksgiving was proclaimed a national holiday by President Abraham Lincoln in 1863. On a day in November, Americans hold special church services, and families get together at Thanksgiving dinners where turkey, with cranberry sauce, sweetcorn, sweet potatoes, pumpkin pie, and whipped cream are served.

Remembrance Day

At 11.00 a.m. on 11th November (the eleventh hour of the eleventh day of the eleventh month) in 1918, an armistice brought the First World War to an end. The war had claimed the lives of ten million soldiers. 11th November was commemorated as Armistice Day, a day for remembering the dead of the Great War. After the Second World War (1939–45) the Sunday nearest 11th November was commemorated as Remembrance Sunday.

On this day wreaths of poppies are laid on war memorials and in gardens of remembrance in countries around the world. Poppies are chosen as a symbol of remembrance because those flowers bloomed on French and Belgian fields even during the fiercest battles of the Great War.

The British monarch lays a wreath at the Cenotaph, the memorial in Whitehall in London, on the morning of Remembrance Sunday, and two minutes' silence is observed from 11 a.m.

In the U.S.A. 11th November is called Veterans' Day. The president or his representative attends a memorial service at the Tomb of the Unknown Soldier in Arlington Cemetery.

Americans also set aside a day each year to remember the men who died in the American Civil War of 1861–5. It is held on 30th May and is called Memorial Day.

How to make a poppy

Here is how to make a beautiful Remembrance Day poppy. You will need:

Some stiff red paper, or white paper painted red on both sides.
A length of stiff wire.
Some strips of green paper or green sellotape.
Two small buttons, one green and one black.

Cut out two pieces of paper the size and shape of the one shown below:

 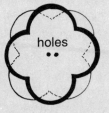

Lay one piece on top of the other, as shown, and then make two small holes through the centre of both pieces.

Push the wire through the green button, then through one of the holes in the pieces of paper, and then through the black button, leaving about 5 cm. (2 in.) protruding. Now bend the wire back through the black button, through the other hole in the pieces of paper and through the green button. Squeeze the buttons together so that the paper is held in place firmly, then wind the wire round and round itself.

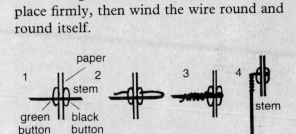

Cover the wire with the strips of green paper or green sellotape and bend the wire to make the stem.

The Day of the Covenant

The Day of the Covenant is an important day for the Afrikaans-speaking people of South Africa. In 1838 the Voortrekkers were at war with the Zulus. The Voortrekkers made a covenant (agreement) with God. They promised to observe that day as a Sunday forever if God granted them victory. They defeated the Zulus at the Battle of Blood River on 16th December 1838, and the victory has been celebrated ever since.

At first the festivities were mainly family affairs, but later 16th December became a public festival day. It used to be called Dingaan's Day (Dingaan was the leader of the Zulus), but was changed to The Day of the Covenant in 1948.

The festival is now observed throughout South Africa. There are church services in the mornings, where the Voortrekkers' vow is read aloud to the standing congregation. The afternoon is given over to festivities.

Another important festival in South Africa is celebrated on Reformation Day, the last Sunday in October. On 31st October 1517, Martin Luther began his public protest against the Catholic Church, so founding the Christian Reformation.

South Africans also celebrate Kruger Day (10th October) and Founders' Day (6th April).

A group of folk dancers in traditional costume celebrate South Africa's Kruger Day in the northern Transvaal.

National Days

Many countries celebrate the day they won independence from a colonial master, or established a new style of government. These days are celebrated not only in the country of origin, but in countries all over the world to which communities have emigrated. We have already mentioned Australia Day, U.S. Independence Day, and Waitangi Day; here are a few more.

4th February, Sri Lankan National Day. The day in 1948 when the country of Ceylon gained independence from British rule. In 1972 it became a republic and changed back to its traditional name of Sri Lanka.

11th February, Japanese National Day. The oldest of all national days, this celebrates the founding of the Japanese nation by its first emperor in 660 B.C.

25th March, Greek Independence Day. The day in 1821 when the Greeks revolted against Turkish rule; they finally won independence in 1832.

5th May, Dutch National Day. This commemorates the day in 1945 when the Netherlands was freed from German occupation near the end of the Second World War.

2nd June, Italian National Day. This is the day in 1946 when Italy voted to become a republic.

1st July, Dominion Day. On this day in 1867 four provinces in Canada formed themselves into the Dominion of Canada. (Later six more provinces joined the Dominion.)

14th July, Bastille Day. The storming of

Canada celebrates its founding in two languages on Dominion Day.

the Bastille (a prison) and the release of prisoners, on this day in 1789, marked the beginning of the French Revolution.

15th August, Indian Independence Day. On this day in 1947 India gained independence after nearly 200 years of British rule.

17th August, Indonesian National Day. On this day in 1945 Indonesia declared independence from Dutch rule.

15th September, Mexican Independence Day. On this day in 1810 Mexico became independent of Spanish rule.

29th October, Turkish Republic Day. This is the day in 1923 when the Turkish Republic was officially declared by Kemal Ataturk, ending the long rule of the Ottoman empire.

7th November, U.S.S.R. National Day. This day celebrates the Bolshevik Revolution of 1917 which ended the Russian monarchy and established the Soviet state.

3
Just for Fun

Some festivals appear to have no real origins at all and are celebrated just for the fun of it. Other festivals are left over from ancient pagan ceremonies which are quite forgotten nowadays. However, they are still fun to celebrate.

St Valentine's Day

St Valentine was a Christian priest who lived in Rome in the third century A.D. The Emperor Claudius had banned marriages, because he thought it prevented men from making good soldiers. Valentine, so it is said, performed secret marriages for lovers who wanted God's blessing for the union. Finally Valentine was captured and brutally murdered on 14th February 269.

Today, 14th February is dedicated to St Valentine and is a special day for lovers. On this day, sweethearts exchange cards with lovehearts on the outside and romantic poems on the inside, as an expression of their love for each other.

Children reach out for a handshake at the Moomba festival in Melbourne.

Moomba Festival

Moomba is an Australian aboriginal word which means something like 'Let's get together and enjoy ourselves.' Every year, for eleven days in March, that is exactly what the people of Melbourne do. They hold sporting events, art exhibitions, plays and concerts. People come from all over Australia to take part in the festival, and look forward especially to the grand parade. Then the crowded streets of the city are filled with colourful floats and marching bands in a procession led by a Moomba King. Children love the trips on the Moomba Show Boat – the *Queen of the Pacific* – on the Yarra River. In the evening, the festival is rounded off with a dazzling firework display.

All Fools' Day

To many people the world over, 1st April is All Fools' Day or April Fools' Day. No one knows for sure how this festival originated, but it was celebrated in France over 400 years ago. Perhaps it was simply a happy and boisterous way of welcoming the spring after the hardships of winter.

All Fools' Day is now the time for sending people on false errands, making them believe in impossible stories, and generally playing tricks.

All Fools' Day is very similar to the Hindu festival of Holi, which is also held around this time (see page 43).

Americans whose forefathers emigrated from Germany still enjoy Oktoberfest in the traditional way.

Oktoberfest

The wedding of King Ludwig I of Bavaria was held on 17th October 1810. The wedding celebrations were so enjoyable

23

Boys and girls at an English school dress up as witches, wizards, and black cats to frighten the unwary on Hallowe'en night.

countries hold celebrations in October which feature Bavarian dancing and singing.

that it was decided to hold the event every year. Now, Oktoberfest lasts sixteen days and includes parades, competitions, and prize-giving, dancing, feasting, and a great deal of beer-drinking.

The biggest celebrations are in Munich. However, German immigrants to Australia and the United States brought Oktoberfest with them. Now many towns in those

Hallowe'en

This celebration owes its origin to the Druids, an ancient religious cult who lived in Britain. Around the end of October they held their New Year festivities. Large fires were lit on hilltops to frighten away witches and other evil spirits. It was also a day for remembering the dead.

In the eighth century, Pope Gregory decided to move the Christian festival of All Hallows (All Saints' Day) to 1st November. Therefore All Hallows E'en (the eve of All Saints' Day) became known as the time when witches and sorcerers roamed about. Young people would play mischievous tricks on the neighbours, and children went around with blackened faces, carrying lamps made from hollowed-out turnips.

Nowadays Hallowe'en is a time for throwing fancy dress parties in which people dress up as witches, ghosts, and

How to make a spooky Hallowe'en witch's hat

For this, you will need:

A circle of black paper about 45 cm (18 inches) in diameter
Another circle of black paper big enough to form the brim of the hat
Glue and sticky tape
Pieces of gold and silver paper

Find the centre of the first circle, and cut a straight line from the centre to the edge.

Form the circle into a cone shape big enough to fit on to your head and then glue or tape the edges together. Now take the other piece of paper and cut a circle in the middle of it the same size as the base of the cone, leaving five or six tabs around the edge as shown in the diagram. This will form the brim of the hat. Glue the tabs on to the inside of the cone. Cut out shapes such as moons, stars, or cats from the gold and silver paper, and stick these on to your hat.

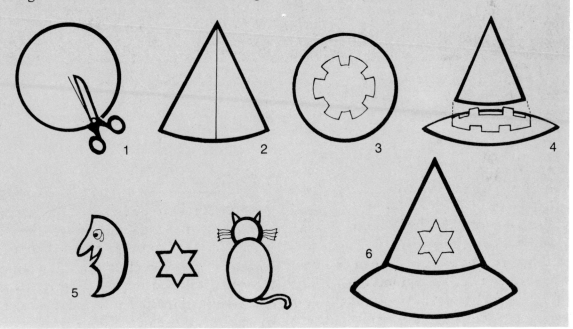

A trick-or-treat disguise in New Jersey.

other scary creatures. In the United States children play 'trick-or-treat'. Dressed in masks, and wearing grotesque costumes, they go from door to door begging sweets, nuts, apples or money. If they are not given a treat, they play a trick on the people.

4

Christian Festivals

Christianity was founded by a young teacher and healer called Jesus Christ, who lived in Palestine nearly 2,000 years ago. Christians believe that he is the Son of God, sent to earth to show people the proper way to live. His message of love and forgiveness has spread all over Europe, North and South America, Australasia, Africa, and large parts of Asia. Therefore Christianity has many forms, and celebrates many different festivals.

Some Christian festivals commemorate things which happened during Jesus's life. Others are dedicated to his followers and are called Saints' Days. The dates of most Christian festivals are decided by the Gregorian calendar. However, some Orthodox Christians (in Greece and parts of the Middle East) use an old calendar and hold their festivals thirteen days later. Other festivals – for example, Easter – are decided by the position of the moon.

Twelfth Night (Epiphany)

Epiphany is an ancient Greek word which means the appearance of a god or supernatural person. Epiphany is held on 6th January, twelve days after Christmas (see page 32). It marks the day when the baby Jesus was first shown to the three wise men who came to see him. It is celebrated with special church services.

To some Orthodox Christians, 6th January is Christmas Eve, because they still use an old calendar which is thirteen days behind the Gregorian calendar.

Epiphany (Twelfth Night) is also the day when, later in his life, Jesus was baptised by John the Baptist, so baptisms are traditionally held on this day. Many Greek people, both in their own country and in communities which have settled in the U.S.A. and Australia, celebrate the 'Blessing of the Waters' on this day. In the

A church play showing the journey of Joseph and Mary to Bethlehem.

evening they celebrate with music, dance, and a feast of salty green cheese, wine, honey cakes, and coffee.

Holy Week and Easter

Holy Week is the most important of all Christian festival times. It commemorates Christ's triumphal entry into Jerusalem, his betrayal, his death, and his resurrection from death.

Holy Week begins with Palm Sunday, so named after the palm leaves which the rejoicing crowds spread before Jesus as he entered the holy city of Jerusalem. special church services are held on this day and crosses made of palm leaves are often handed out to members of the congregation.

The Thursday of Holy Week is called Maundy Thursday and marks the day on which Jesus ate the last Passover supper (see page oo) with his twelve disciples. At the supper he washed their feet, and it later became the custom for the kings and queens of England to wash the feet of poor

28

people on this day, and to give them gifts. This act of giving survives to this day when 'Maundy Money' is presented to as many poor people as there are years in the monarch's age.

Good Friday is the day on which people remember Jesus Christ's death by crucifixion. Special services are held in Christian churches, and some people eat no meat on this day. They do eat hot cross buns, though. These are sweet fruit buns marked on top with the sign of the cross, which represents the cross on which Jesus was executed, and they are warmed in the oven before eating.

Good Friday is followed by Holy Saturday. In Los Angeles, U.S.A., a 'blessing of the animals' ceremony takes place on this day. In the Mexican shopping area of Olvera Street, children bring their pets to be blessed by the priest.

Holy Week ends on Saturday, and the following day is Easter Day. Easter Sunday is one of the most important festivals in the

How to make an Easter basket

The Easter hare or Easter bunny always carries his eggs in an Easter basket. To make one for yourself you will need:

A large rectangle and a strip of stiff card which you have painted with water-colours.
Scissors, glue, and stapler.

Cut even slits in one of the long edges of the rectangle about one-third the width.

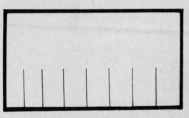

Bend the paper to make a cylinder and staple the edges together.

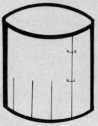

Fold in the cut strips and glue them together.

Glue or staple the strip to make a handle.

You can fill your basket with coloured, hard-boiled eggs on a bed of straw or crumpled paper.

You can colour hard-boiled eggs either by adding food dyes to the water when you boil them, or by making your own dyes. Onion skins in the water will colour the eggs yellow. Beetroot juice will colour them pink. Moss or birch leaves will colour them green.

whole Christian calendar. On this day, bells rings out joyously from churches all over the world in celebration of Jesus rising from the dead.

The giving of eggs (a symbol of birth and life) has long been the custom on this day. In some countries the eggs are said to be delivered by an Easter hare or Easter bunny. Egg-rolling races are often held on this day or on Easter Monday. The most famous takes place on the lawns of the White House, the home of the U.S. President in Washington D.C.

Irish Americans dress 'in the green' to celebrate St Patrick's Day in Georgia.

St Patrick's Day

St Patrick is the patron saint of Ireland, and St Patrick's Day on 17th March is a great day of celebration for Irish people everywhere. St Patrick is believed to have been born in England in about A.D. 389. He was sent to Ireland to convert the people to the Catholic faith.

Many legends are connected with his name. He is said to have taken the three-leaved shamrock (now the emblem of Ireland) as a symbol of the Holy Trinity of the Christian religion – the Father, the Son, and the Holy Ghost. He is also believed to have driven all the snakes out of Ireland, and to have taught the Irish the secrets of

New Orleans bursts into life as the Mardi Gras festival brings thousands of marchers and dancers out on to the streets.

distillation. His day has now become one on which pubs and clubs in Ireland and in the Irish quarters of cities around the world are full to the brim. People wear shamrocks and dress 'in the green', which is the traditional colour of Ireland. In Chicago, in the United States, green dye is poured into the Chicago River. In New York, a green line is painted down the middle of the streets to mark the route of the St Patrick's Day Parade.

Shrove Tuesday and Mardi Gras

Shrove Tuesday is the last day before Lent, a forty-day fast period. It takes its name from the old word 'shrive' meaning forgiveness, for people would confess their sins on this day.

31

Shrove Tuesday was the day on which all the eggs, fats, and other foods forbidden during Lent were eaten. So it became the tradition in Britain to make these foods into pancakes. The custom survives today, both in Britain and in other countries where British people have settled. Pancakes are made, and in some places pancake races are held between competing teams of women who must run a certain distance while tossing a pancake from the frying pan several times in the air. There is even an international pancake race between the women of Olney, in Buckinghamshire, England, and those of Liberal, in Kansas. The times of the competitors are recorded and the results relayed by 'phone across the Atlantic.

A more spectacular festival, held in New Orleans in the United States, comes to a noisy end on Shrove Tuesday. It is called Mardi Gras, which is French for 'Fat Tuesday'. On the night of Shrove Tuesday the streets of the city are filled with hundreds of gaily coloured floats, innumerable bands, and thousands of marchers and dancers. Everyone wears wonderful costumes of clowns, fabulous beasts, comic strip characters, or famous Americans.

Mothering Sunday

The fourth Sunday in Lent has long been a special day to Christians. At one time, it was the day when people from outlying parishes visited their nearest Cathedral, their 'mother church'. Later this custom was extended and applied to the mother of the family as well. Young men and women would visit their mothers on this day, usually bringing with them a gift of a bunch of violets or a simnel cake.

The custom died out in Britain, but during the Second World War (1939–45) visiting American soldiers, who had their own Mother's day, revived the custom in Britain. British people resumed celebrating the fourth Sunday in Lent as Mothering Sunday, when mothers are brought gifts and given a rest from the household chores. In the United States, Australia, New Zealand, and Canada, Mother's Day is celebrated on the second Sunday in May.

Christmas

Christmas, on 25th December, is the most festive of all Christian holidays. It celebrates the birth of Jesus almost 2,000 years ago. Jesus's parents, Joseph and Mary, travelled to Bethlehem to be enrolled, or counted by the Romans who ruled Israel at that time. Because all the inns in the town were full, they had to spend the night in a stable. It was there that the baby Jesus was born.

The preparation for the modern celebration of Christmas begins four weeks beforehand with Advent. Advent means 'coming' or 'happening'. People often buy Advent calendars to mark off the days before Christ's 'coming' on Christmas Day. A few days before Christmas people begin decorating their houses with holly and paper chains. A small fir tree is planted in a tub and decorated with tinsel and electric lights. Songs celebrating Christ-mas, called carols, are sung by choirs who go from house to house collecting money for charity. Across America, the big department stores feature huge choirs of carol singers to cheer the Christmas shoppers.

How to make a Christmas cracker

To make your own crackers to pull at your Christmas dinner you will need:

Toilet rolls, two for each cracker
Crepe paper
Cracker bangs, which you can buy from novelty shops
Nuts or sweets, for the gifts
Crepe paper
Pretty pictures which you can cut from old Christmas cards
Scissors and glue
Rubber bands Paper doilies Thin ribbons

Take one toilet roll and lay the cracker bang in it so that it sticks out of each end.

cracker bang

Take another toilet roll, cut it in half and lay the halves at each end of the main one.

Dab some glue around the rolls and then roll them all up in the crepe paper.

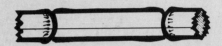

Fix a rubber band between the rolls at one end to pull in the crepe paper. Pop your gift or sweet inside and fasten the other end. Under the rubber band, slightly weaken the crepe paper with a circle of small slits at intervals. Cut the crepe paper at each end to make a jagged edge.

Glue some pieces of paper doily at each end to cover up the join, and stick a pretty picture in the middle. Tie ribbons to cover the rubber bands.

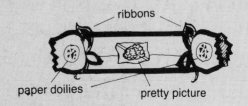
ribbons
paper doilies
pretty picture

A gaily lit Christmas tree brightens up the grey buildings of New York.

in red, who travels down from the North Pole in a sleigh drawn by reindeer, to give presents to all good children.

On Christmas Day itself, special services are held in the morning in all Christian churches. Later, families get together for a traditional meal of roast turkey followed by hot mince pies, Christmas pudding, and Christmas cake. In countries like Australia, where Christmas falls in the middle of summer, people often eat turkey sandwiches on the beach under the hot sun. Houses remain decorated until after the New Year, but it is thought unlucky to leave the decorations up after Twelfth Night (see page 27).

On Christmas Eve (or on another night in some countries), children put out stockings or shoes under the Christmas tree or by their beds for Father Christmas to fill with presents. Father Christmas (Santa Claus) is seen as a jolly, fat man, dressed all

Other Christian Festivals

There are many other Christian festivals and Saints' Days which are held at different times of the year. Here is a list of some of them:

Candlemas is the day in February when candles (symbols of Christ as 'the light of the world') are blessed and distributed to the congregation in special church services.

St David's Day on 1st March is dedicated to the patron saint of Wales.

The Annunciation of the Blessed Virgin Mary commemorates the day when the Angel Gabriel told the Virgin Mary that she was going to give birth to Jesus. It is on 25th March.

St George's Day on 23rd April is dedicated to the patron saint of England.

Australians in shirtsleeves celebrate their mid-summer Christmas in Adelaide.

The fortieth day after Easter is celebrated as *Ascension Day*, the day on which the spirit of the resurrected Christ ascended to heaven.

Pentecost (Whitsun) is celebrated in May. It is the day when the followers of Jesus received the Holy Spirit, a power which came over them all and encouraged them to go out and teach the word of Jesus.

The *Feast of Our Lady of Czestochowa* on 3rd May is an important day for Polish Christians.

Trinity Sunday in May is a day set aside by Christians for remembering that God is really three persons – the Father, the Son and the Holy Spirit.

On 2nd November, prayers are offered for the souls of people who have died, in the ceremony of *All Souls' Day*.

St Andrew's Day on 30th November is dedicated to the patron saint of Scotland.

35

5
Jewish Festivals

The religion of Jewish people is called Judaism. Judaism began almost 4,000 years ago with a man called Abraham. In return for obedience and worship, God would allow Abraham and his descendants to live in the land of Canaan (now called Israel), where a great nation would be founded.

The Jews, like the Christians and Muslims, believe in only one God. Their religion is based upon their holy books – the Torah and the Talmud. Since 1948 Jews have had a country of their own – Israel – in which to build a nation. Although many Jews now live in Israel, millions still live in various different countries around the world.

The dates of Jewish festivals are determined by their own religious calendar, which is a lunisolar calendar. This means that Jewish festivals are not held on the same date in the year, but can vary by as much as a month. The calendar on page 57 tells you the approximate time of year when Jewish festivals fall.

Purim

Purim is one of the most joyous of all Jewish festivals. It commemorates the day, 2400 years ago, when the Jews were saved from execution by Haman, a Minister of King Ahasuerus. Eventually it was Haman himself, and his sons, who were executed by the King.

Purim falls on a day in February or March. Delicacies called Haman's ear or Haman's pocket are eaten. Jews in the United States burn an effigy of Haman, in a festival which includes the election of a Purim King or Purim Rabbi. A 'Queen Esther' is elected in a Purim carnival beauty contest. In schools and community centres Purim plays are acted.

There is even boisterousness in the Jewish temple – the Synagogue. The book

Children in fancy dress celebrate Purim in the streets of Jerusalem.

36

of Esther is read to the gathering, and whenever Haman's name is mentioned children whirl rattles, called 'greggers', and stamp their feet.

Passover (Pesach)

Passover is a Jewish spring festival in March or April which lasts for eight days. The first two and the last two days are official religious holidays, when Jewish schools, shops and offices are closed. The festival recalls the Jews' escape from slavery in Egypt in about 1250 B.C., and it also celebrates the harvest of winter-sown barley.

During Passover, families get together for a special commemorative meal called the Seder. At the Seder, the youngest child present asks the father four questions. In answering these questions, the story of the Jews' deliverance is told.

Four glasses of wine are drunk as a

A table is laid for the Seder meal on the first night of Passover.

How to make Charoses

It is very easy to make Charoses. All you have to do is chop finely, or mince together, the following ingredients:

Two medium sized apples (after first peeling them and removing the cores)
A few dates, without the stones
One tablespoon of candied peel
Nine tablespoons of candied peel
Half teacup of peeled almonds

Once you have formed these into a paste, add cinnamon to taste.

symbol of rejoicing, and these symbolic foods are laid out:

Parsley, celery or potatoes, as a reminder of the coming of spring. They are dipped in salt water before being eaten as a symbol of the tears shed by the Jews while in captivity, and also of the Red Sea, which parted and allowed them to escape the pursuing soldiers.

Bitter herbs are eaten to bring tears to the eyes and remind the eater of the tears of the Jews. The bitter herbs are, however, first dipped in a sweet paste called Charoses. This paste is a reminder of the mortar which the Jewish slaves used to build the Egyptian Pharoahs' cities. The bitter and sweet mixture also symbolizes the Jews' happy escape after their years of slavery.

On the table, but not eaten, is the roasted bone of a lamb to serve as a reminder of the lambs the Jews sacrificed on the eve of their escape.

Passover celebrates the Jews' escape from slavery in Egypt. This is a Passover supper being held on a kibbutz in Israel.

Also on the table is a roasted egg, which represents the festival sacrifice.

Finally, there are three whole matzohs (unleavened loaves). These are loaves which have not been allowed to rise because, as the story tells, there was no time on the day of their escape for the Jews to allow the bread to rise.

Jewish New Year and Day of Atonement

Rosh Hashanah is the Jewish New Year which falls in September or October. It is the beginning of a ten-day period of penitence before God. Penitence means being sorry for any wrong things you have done. On Rosh Hashanah, Jews also celebrate God's creation of the world, and the story of Abraham. The blowing of a horn, called a Shofar, reminds them of the

39

ram which was sacrificed instead of Abraham's son, Isaac.

On New Year's Eve Jews eat sweet foods, like apple dipped in honey, honey cake, honey cookies, and sweet potato pudding. This symbolizes their wish for a 'sweet' year. The customary greeting on this day is 'May you be inscribed for a good year,' for Jews believe that every Jew's destiny has been written down by God on this day.

Yom Kippur, the Day of Atonement, comes at the end of the ten days of penitence. It is the day when Jews make amends for all the sins they might have committed during the year. Adults fast

The blowing of a ram's horn on Rosh Hashanah reminds Jews of Abraham's sacrifice of the ram.

A Jewish New Year recipe – Apple and honey compote

This is an easy dish to make. All you need to make six helpings is:

2 lb of baking apples
2 tablespoons of lemon juice
1 cup of honey
$\frac{1}{4}$ teaspoon of nutmeg
$\frac{1}{4}$ cup of white wine or orange juice

Peel the apples and take out the cores. Then cut them up into quarters, and place in a baking dish. Mix together the lemon juice, honey, nutmeg, and wine or orange juice. Pour this mixture over the apples, and bake uncovered in an oven at 375°F for 45 minutes, basting the apples every so often.

A sukkot is erected in a synagogue during the Rejoicing of the Law.

from sundown to sunset, neither eating nor drinking, and spend most of the day at prayer in the synagogue.

Sukkot and Rejoicing of the Law

Sukkot was originally a harvest festival, but later it also came to commemorate the journey of the Jews through the wilderness during their flight from slavery in Egypt. During this time they stayed in temporary dwelling places called Sukkot, and it is from these that the festival gets its name today.

Nowadays Sukkot are built in synagogues and gardens during this nine-day festival. They are decorated with leafy branches, flowers, and fruit. Meals and other family activities take place within them.

Jews from Bokhara in the Soviet Union bring their colourful traditions to Simchat Torah in Tel Aviv.

When the Temple's perpetual lamp was about to be lit, however, only one day's supply of holy oil could be found. Legend tells how, nevertheless, the oil lasted eight days – long enough for more oil to be prepared. Jewish people now celebrate Chanukah in memory of this miracle.

A light is kindled on the first day of the festival, two on the second, and so on until eight lights are kindled on the eighth day. During the Chanukah period Jewish homes are gaily decorated, gifts are exchanged, and parties are held. Festive meals often include latkes – traditional potato pancakes.

The ninth day of Sukkot is called Simchat Torah, Rejoicing of the Torah (the Torah is the Jewish law). The scrolls of the Torah are carried seven times around the synagogue, while people sing and dance, and children carry flags at the end of sticks garnished with apples.

Chanukah

Chanukah is an eight-day festival in December. It recalls a time when Jerusalem was ruled over by the Greeks, who forced the Jews to worship their gods.

The Jews, led by Judas Maccabaeus, mounted a successful revolt against this persecution, entered Jerusalem in 165 B.C., and cleansed the Jewish temple there.

Other Jewish Festivals

Here are some other important festivals which are celebrated by Jewish people all round the world:

In January or February people celebrate *Tu B' Shevat*, the New Year for Trees, by planting new trees.

Israel Independence Day falls in April or May. Lights are kindled in commemoration of the rebirth of the Jewish state of Israel.

Shavuot, or Pentecost (also called the Feast of Weeks), is held in May. It commemorates God's gift of the Ten Commandments to the great Israelite leader Moses.

The fast day of *Tishah-B'Av* is held in July. It commemorates the destruction of the Temples in Jerusalem, and other tragedies in Jewish history.

6
Hindu Festivals

Hinduism began to develop between four and five thousand years ago. Hindus believe in one Supreme God, but they believe God can have many forms. The three most important forms are Brahma, the Creator of the universe; Vishnu, the Preserver, who looks after the universe; and Shiva, the Destroyer, who has the power to bring creation to an end.

Most Hindus live in India, but large numbers have emigrated to South Africa, East Africa, Britain, and other countries. Hindu festivals mostly celebrate events in the lives of their gods, especially Krishna and Rama. Like the Jews, the Hindus use a lunisolar calendar to work out the dates for their festivals, so they do not occur on the same Gregorian calendar date each year.

Holi

The spring festival of Holi falls in March. It is a happy, joyous, and rather mischievous celebration which has ancient origins. One day Lord Krishna, the last incarnation of Vishnu, was celebrating the first full moon of the spring with some of his friends. There was music, song, and dance, and everyone was enjoying themselves. Krishna then began throwing coloured powder over one of the girls, a princess called Radha.

Holi is still a time for mischievous pranks, and some Hindus still go as far as to

Coloured powders for sale at Holi.

43

in the evenings. In the temples special foods are offered to God – things like almonds, ground nuts, and fruit. Special foods are eaten, too, like roasted coconut, the Hindu symbol of fertility. It is also a time for retelling all the stories of Lord Krishna.

Near Mathura, in northern India, there is a mock duel between the men of Nandgaon (home of Krishna), and the women of Barsana (home of Radha, Krishna's consort). The women throw powder over the men, and the men reply the following day.

Sikhs have a similar festival called Hola, which they celebrate about the same time as Holi. However, they take the festival rather more seriously, and mischievous pranks are not played.

An Indian girl ties a silken amulet on her brother's wrist during the festival of Rakshabandhan.

throw coloured powder over each other. There is fun and dancing, youngsters can be rude to their elders, and bonfires are lit

Rakshabandhan

Rakshabandhan is a festival for Hindu brothers and sisters. It falls on the full moon during the Hindu month of Shravana, which falls in July or August. On this day girls tie a bracelet called a rakhi of coloured cotton or silk threads around the wrist of their brother. They also mark their forehead with coloured vermilion. The rakhi symbolizes the tie that holds brother and sister together, and obliges the brother to look after his sister. In return for this honour the brother gives to his sister a present such as clothing, jewellery, or money.

44

Janam Ashtami

On midnight of this day in August the Hindu Lord Krishna was born, and it is a day of fasting for all Hindus including children. In India, the fasting continues until midnight. In other countries where Hindus have settled, fasting ends at the hour equivalent to midnight in India. Prayers are held all night in Hindu temples, and scenes from the early life of Krishna are acted out in plays. Sometimes the temple holds an image of the infant Krishna, laid in a cradle. Presents of sweets are given to the baby.

Diwali

Diwali is the Hindu New Year festival held in October or November. It is the time when Lakshmi, the goddess of prosperity, visits homes lit by many lamps. Bengalis call Lakshmi by the name of Kali, so the festival is also known as Kali Puja.

Diwali lasts five days, though only the third day is Diwali proper. This day commemorates Lord Rama's return to his kingdom with his wife, Sita, following her rescue from the evil Ravana. He was greeted by his subjects who each carried a small clay lamp, called a diwa or deepa.

On Diwali today, diwa are ceremonially lit, houses are beautifully illuminated, friends and relatives visit each other to exchange presents and cards, and there is feasting, fireworks, and prayer in the

Diwali lamp

You can make a simple lamp from clay to decorate your classroom on Diwali.

Roll out a piece of clay to a thickness of about 5 mm ($\frac{3}{16}$ in.). Cut two small oval shapes from the clay, one slightly larger than the other. Scratch the centres of the ovals to make two rough surfaces. Join the rough surfaces together using a little slurry (clay mixed with water) so that the small oval lies on top of the larger one.

scratch surface

Carefully turn up the edges of the smaller oval, and make a lip at one end. Turn up the edges of the larger oval all the way round.

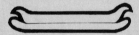

Fire your lamp. Place a night light or short piece of candle inside and light it.

temple. As it is also the beginning of the New Year it is a time when Hindu businessmen pray for future prosperity.

Dussehra

Dussehra celebrates the victory of Lord Rama over the demon king Ravana, who had stolen Rama's wife. Rama killed Ravana with the help of a magic arrow given to him by the wise magician Agastya. The arrow was made from fire and sunlight and weighed as much as a mountain.

Dussehra is one of the most popular and widely celebrated of all the Hindu festivals. In India, the festivities last for ten days during September or October, but in other parts of the world where Hindus live the period is often shortened to four or five days. Processions are held; there is dancing; and families get together and exchange gifts. It is also a time when brides and engaged couples are presented with gifts.

Other Hindu Festivals

Because Hindus have many different forms of God, they have many, many festivals too. Here are some other festivals which Hindus like to celebrate:

In February there are three festivals. *Shiva Ratri* (the Dance of the Shiva festival) commemorates the God Shiva as the Lord of the Dance. *Sarasvati Puja* is a festival dedicated to Sarasvati, the wife of Brahma, and a patroness of literature and music. The *Birthday of Sri Ramakrishna* celebrates the birth of this Hindu saint of the nineteenth century.

Ram Navmi, in March, celebrates the birthday of Lord Rama.

Ratha Yatra is a spectacular festival celebrated in May or June at Puri and other places in India. It is in honour of Jagannath, the Lord of the Universe.

A giant effigy of the demon king Ravana is burned on the tenth day of Dussehra.

In Bengal the warrior goddess Durga is honoured at Dussehra.

46

7

Muslim Festivals

The religion of Muslim people is called Islam. Islam means 'submission' to the will of God, who they call Allah. Muslims believe that the will of Allah was revealed through his prophet, Muhammed, who lived in Arabia in the sixth and seventh centuries A.D. One night, when Muhammed was about forty years old, he was visited by the angel Gabriel and told to 'preach in the name of the Lord, the Creator'.

This is how Muhammed's life of teaching began. At first, Islam made little headway. In 622, Muhammed was forced to flee the holy city of Mecca where he was preaching and go to Medina. There he gathered about him a group of loyal followers and, after beating off a number of attacks, he returned to Mecca in triumph in 630. After this, Islam began to spread, and by A.D. 750, the Muslim Empire stretched throughout the Middle East to the border with India and west across North Africa and into Spain and France.

Nowadays, most Muslims live in the Arab countries of the Middle East and North Africa, Iran, Afghanistan, India, Pakistan, Bangladesh, the southern U.S.S.R., and China. Smaller communities are found in most countries.

There are five pillars of Islam. They are: Belief in the oneness of God (Allah) and the Prophet Muhammed; Prayers, which must be held five times a day; Fasting during the month of Ramadan; Zakat (the compulsory giving of charity); Pilgrimage to Mecca at least once in a lifetime.

The dates for Muslim festivals are determined by their lunar calendar. There is no adjustment to keep the lunar year in line with the solar year, therefore Muslim festivals move throughout the seasons, returning to about the same place in the Gregorian calendar every $32\frac{1}{2}$ years. The approximate dates for the Muslim festivals from 1984 to 1990 are shown on the calendar on page 57).

For Muslims an unalterable part of every festival is a gathering for prayers at the mosque. This one is in Istanbul, Turkey.

Ramadan and Eid-Ul-Fitr

Ramadan is the ninth month of the Muslim year. During this month, all Muslims fast between the hours of sunrise and sunset. Fasting encourages physical and mental self-denial, and allows rich people to experience the misery of poverty.

On the twenty-seventh day of Ramadan there is a special night called Lailat-Ul-Qadr, the 'Night of Power'. This commemorates the time of the first revelation from Allah, which Muhammed received through the angel Gabriel. Muslims stay awake on this night, reciting the Koran (the holy book) and saying prayers.

Eid-Ul-Fitr, the 'small Eid', marks the end of Ramadan. It is a joyous occasion when families and friends send each other greeting cards, visit each other, wear new clothes, and share specially prepared food and drink. Children look forward to receiving gifts from the older members of the family. Muslim men attend the Eid prayer at the mosque. Muslim women usually stay at home to pray, although some will also go to the mosque and pray in a different part from the men.

How to make an Eid card

To make a card to send to a Muslim friend on Eid-Ul-Fitr or Eid-Ul-Adha, you will need:

A piece of stiff white paper measuring 35 cm × 18 cm (14 in × 7 in)
Scissors
Some colouring pencils, felt-tipped pens, or poster paints

Fold the card over twice to make a rectangle 17.5 cm × 9 cm (7 in × 3½ in).

Decorate the front of the card with an Islamic design or a picture of an Islamic building, such as a mosque. You could even try copying an Islamic painting from a book, or, of course, you could cut one out of a magazine and glue it on to the front.

Inside, write: 'Eid Greetings' and your friend's name. If your friend speaks Urdu, the main language of Pakistan, you could write 'Eid-Ul-Fitr Mubarak' or 'Eid-Ul-Adha Mubarak'.

Eid-Ul-Adha

Eid-Ul-Adha, the 'great Eid', is a joyous worldwide festival which falls seventy days after Ramadan and at the end of the pilgrimage to Mecca. Lasting four days, the festival has the same origins as the Jewish festival of Rosh Hashanah (see page 39). It commemorates the sacrifice of a ram in place of the son of Ibrahim (whom Jews call Abraham).

After prayers in the mosque on the first morning of Eid-Ul-Adha, an animal is sacrificed. Usually the animal is a lamb, although it could be a goat, a cow, or a camel. The animal is then divided into three. One piece goes to the man who has made the sacrifice, and his family. The second piece is given to friends and neighbours (even if they are not Muslims). The third piece is given to the poor.

Other Muslim Festivals

Like Lailat-Ul-Qadr, most of the other Muslim festivals commemorate things which happened during the life of the Prophet Muhammed.

Lailat-Ul-Isra Wal Mi'Raj, the Night of the Journey and the Ascension, is the night when Muslims remember the journey of Muhammed from Mecca to Jerusalem, and his ascent to heaven.

Lailat-Ul-Bara'h, the Night of Forgiveness, is the time when Muslims seek forgiveness from God, and when their fate for the coming year is decided.

From the minarets of every mosque the faithful are called to prayer during Ramadan.

The Day of Hijrah is the first day of the Islamic New Year, and commemorates the migration of the Prophet Muhammed from Mecca to Medina.

Meelad (or *Mawlid*)-*Ul-Nabi* celebrates the birth of Muhammed on 20th August 570. This falls on 12th Rabi-Ul-Awal in the Muslim calendar.

8

Sikh Festivals

Sikhism was founded in the Punjab region of north-west India in the late fifteenth century by Guru Nanak. The title 'Guru' means religious teacher.

Guru Nanak was born a Hindu in a village called Talwandi. He grew up in the midst of much poverty and conflict between Hindus and Muslims. Sikhism arose from his belief that all men and women are equal in the eyes of God. Two of his sayings illustrate his life. They are:

'There is neither Muslim nor Hindu.'

'To love God, you must first learn to love each other.'

After Guru Nanak came nine other gurus. The tenth and last guru was Guru Gobind Singh. He was assassinated in 1708, and since then the place of Sikh guru has been taken by the Sikh holy book, the Granth Sahib.

Gurpurbs

Sikhs celebrate the births and deaths of the Gurus with a Gurpurb. The four most regularly celebrated are the birthdays of Guru Nanak and Guru Gobind Singh, and the days when Guru Arjan and Guru Tegh Bahadur were martyred for their beliefs.

Although all gurpurbs are dedicated to different gurus, they all have two rituals in common. The first is the continuous reading of the Granth Sahib. The reading begins in the Gurdwara (the Sikh temple) two days before the actual date for the celebration. The second is the special service in the Gurdwara devoted to the particular Guru. Hymns are sung, with the singers playing traditional musical instruments like the tabla. After the service the congregation will be invited to stay for a special free meal, called 'langar'.

In Britain the celebrations usually take place during the weekend after the anniversary, unless it happens to fall on a Sunday.

Often the celebrations include a procession, where the Granth Sahib is carried high. Sikhs wish each other 'Happy Guru Nanak Birthday' or 'Happy Guru Gobind Singh Birthday'.

Baisakhi

Baisakhi Day is an ancient harvest festival. It is widely celebrated in April all over India, but is a particularly important day for Sikhs. On this day in 1699 Guru Gobind Singh, their tenth and last guru, baptised his first batch of five disciples and established the Order of 'Khalsa'.

With the founding of the Khalsa, Guru Gobind Singh initiated the wearing of the five symbols of Sikhism, which is still practised to this day. These symbols are: the Kangha (a wooden comb); Kara (a steel bracelet); Kirpan (a sword); Kaccha (a pair of shorts); and Kesh (long hair, often kept in place with a turban).

Today, the Baisakhi festival is a mixture of entertainment and serious worship. In the Sikh temple, the gurdwara, the Granth Sahib is read continuously for two days before Baisakhi. On the day itself prayers are said, and accounts of Sikh history are read. New members are initiated into Khalsa. Sikhs share sweets and savouries and offer charity, and there are often processions in the steets.

An elephant takes part in a Punjab parade to commemorate the death of the Sikh martyr Guru Tegh Bahadur.

Diwali

Sikhs share with Hindus in the festival of Diwali (see page 45), because it celebrates the release of their sixth Guru, Guru Hargobind, from imprisonment at Gwalior Fort, and his arrival at the famous Golden Temple of Amritsar. On this day the Golden Temple is lavishly illuminated, and Sikhs everywhere celebrate with prayer, lights, fireworks, and feasting.

9
Chinese and Buddhist Festivals

Since China became a communist country in 1949 the ancient religious festivals have diminished. However, there are Chinese people living all over the world. The old festivals are still celebrated in certain countries of south-east Asia, and in the Chinese quarters of cities in many other countries including Australia, the United States, and Britain.

Chinese religion is very old. One of its most important aspects is reverence for dead ancestors – parents, grandparents, great-grandparents and so on. Therefore many of the Chinese festivals are dedicated to ancestors. The Chinese calendar is lunisolar, therefore the dates of their festivals vary by as much as a few weeks from year to year.

Ching Ming

This spring festival, which usually falls in April, is a time when Chinese people think about their dead ancestors. For three days before Ching Ming, they eat no hot food and light no fires. On the day itself, they visit their ancestors' graves. There they plant flowers, tidy up the graves, and offer food and wine, clothes and furniture. These are later burned in the hope that the 'spirit' of the burnt offering will reach their dead ancestors.

Time of Sending Winter Clothes to Ancestors

This festival falls in November or thereabouts. Again, graves are cleaned and gifts are left. The gifts used to be suits of winter clothes made of paper. These would be burned at the grave as an offering to the spirits. Later, the gifts were changed to 'spirit money' wrapped in plain paper. These gifts were burned in the same way.

Chinese families in Hong Kong visit the graves of their dead ancestors to offer food and clothes during the spring festival of Ching Ming.

Buddhism was founded by an Indian prince about 2,500 years ago. It is an important religion in Sri Lanka, Burma, Thailand, South Korea, Japan, and in some other countries.

The Buddha was born Siddhartha Gautama in the sixth century B.C. The son of a wealthy ruler, he was for many years sheltered from all poverty, suffering and death. However, as a young man, he decided to turn away from his life of luxury. He left his palace to become a yogi. He starved himself, slept in graveyards, and generally subjected his body to much hardship. But he realised that this would lead only to death, so he bathed, took a little food, and sat down to meditate under the Bodhi tree. He was determined to find an answer to his question, 'What is the cause of suffering, and is there a way of ending it?' Then, at the age of 35, he emerged with a perfect understanding of the meaning of life. The next forty-five years he spent teaching his way of thinking.

Wisteria, iris, and plum decorate a cart during Japan's Aoi Matsuri festival.

Birth, Enlightenment, and Death of Buddha

The most important Buddhist festivals celebrate the Buddha's birth, his 'enlightenment', and his death. Some Buddhists (the Mahayana Buddhists) celebrate these events in three festivals held in April, December and February. Other Buddhists (the Theravada Buddhists) celebrate them in one festival held in the lunar month of Vesakha, which usually falls in May. This festival they call Wesak. In Japan, the birthday always falls on 8th April.

Buddhists decorate their houses with lanterns and garlands, and give presents. Food and alms are distributed to monks and nuns, and flowers are placed before statues of the Buddha. Birds are released from their cages as a symbol of the Buddha's love for all living things.

Other Buddhist Festivals

Other important festivals include Asalha Puja, which is held in June or July and commemorates the day when the Buddha preached his first sermon. Kathina is a ceremony often held in October or November when Buddhists present gifts, often of cloth, to their monks.

10
Calendar of Festivals

Here is a list of the dates (according to the Gregorian calendar) for all festivals mentioned in this book. Festivals which have no fixed dates, or which are determined by other calendars, vary in date from year to year and have therefore been placed in the Gregorian months in which they most usually fall. Estimated dates of Muslim festivals, which have no correspondence with the Gregorian calendar, have been shown up to the year 1990. For accurate dates of all movable festivals you could enquire at your local church, temple, mosque, gurdwara, or synagogue, or at the embassy or high commission of a country where the religion is widely practised. A calendar of the world's religions is published annually by The Commission for Racial Equality, Elliott House, 10–12 Allington Street, London SW1E 5EH, England. There is no charge, but a stamped addressed envelope must be supplied.

January

Fixed festivals

1st   New Year
2nd   Second New Year's Day
6th   Epiphany
7th   Christmas Day (for some Greek Orthodox Christians)
26th Australia Day

Movable festivals

Wheat Harvest in Australia
Chinese New Year
New Year for Trees

February

Fixed festivals

4th   Sri Lankan National Day
6th   Waitangi Day
11th Japanese National Day
12th Abraham Lincoln's Birthday
14th St Valentine's Day
22nd George Washington's Birthday

Movable festivals

Candlemas
Shrove Tuesday
Mardi Gras
Purim

Shiva Ratri
Sarasvati Puja
Sri Ramakrishna's Birthday
Buddha's Death (for Mahayana Buddhists)

March

Fixed festivals

1st   St David's Day
12th   Canberra Day
17th   St Patrick's Day
25th   Annunciation of the Blessed Virgin Mary
25th   Greek Independence Day

Movable festivals

Moomba Festival
Apple Harvest in Tasmania
Holi
Hola
Mothering Sunday in Britain
Palm Sunday
Maundy Thursday
Good Friday
Holy Saturday
Easter
Passover
Ram Navmi
Lailat-Ul-Isra Wal Mi'Raj (in 1988, 1989, 1990)
Ramadan begins (in 1990)
Lailat-Ul-Bara'h (in 1989, 1990)

April

Fixed festivals

1st   All Fools' Day
6th   Founder's Day in South Africa
23rd   St George's Day
25th   ANZAC Day

Movable festivals

Grape Harvest in South Australia

Baisakhi
Ching Ming
Buddha's Birthday (for Mahayana Buddhists)
Ramadan begins (in 1987, 1988, 1989)
Lailat-Ul-Isra Wal Mi'Raj (in 1984 1985, 1986, 1987)
Lailat-Ul-Qadr (in 1990)
Eid-Ul-Fitr (in 1990)
Lailat-Ul-Bara'h (in 1986, 1987, 1988)

May

Fixed festivals

1st   May Day
1st   Labour Day
1st   Loyalty Day
3rd   Feast of Our Lady of Czestochowa
5th   Dutch National Day
30th   Memorial Day in U.S.A.

Movable festivals

Israel Independence Day
Mother's Day in U.S., New Zealand, Australia, and Canada
Ascension Day
Trinity Sunday
Shavuot (Pentecost)
Whitsun (Pentecost)
Wesak (for Theravada Buddhists)
Ramadan begins (in 1984, 1985, 1986)
Lailat-Ul-Qadr (in 1987, 1988, 1989)
Eid-Ul-Fitr (in 1987, 1988, 1989)
Lailat-Ul-Bara'h (in 1984, 1985)
Ratha Yatra
Aoi Matsuri

June

Fixed festivals

2nd   Italian National Day

Movable festivals

Foundation Day in Western Australia
Corpus Christi

Martyrdom of Guru Arjan Dev
Asalha Puja
Lailat-Ul-Qadr (in 1984, 1985, 1986)
Eid-Ul-Fitr (in 1984, 1985, 1986)

July

Fixed festivals

1st   Dominion Day
4th   U.S. Independence Day
14th   Bastille Day

Movable festivals
Aboriginal Day
Tishah-B'Av
Rakshabandhan
Eid-Ul-Adha (in 1988, 1989, 1990)

August

Fixed festivals

15th   Indian Independence Day
17th   Indonesian National Day

Movable festivals
Janam Ashtami
Eid-Ul-Adha (in 1985, 1986, 1987)
Day of Hijrah (in 1988, 1989, 1990)

September

Fixed festivals
16th   Mexican Independence Day

Movable festivals
Jewish New Year and Day of Atonement
Sukkot and Rejoicing of the Law
Harvest
Dussehra
Eid-Ul-Adha (in 1984)
Meelad-Ul-Nabi (in 1990)
Day of Hijrah (in 1985, 1986, 1987)

October

Fixed festivals

10th   Kruger Day

12th   Columbus Day
29th   Turkish Republic Day
31st   Hallowe'en

Movable festivals
Oktoberfest
Kathina
Diwali
Meelad-Ul-Nabi (in 1987, 1988, 1989)
Reformation Day
Day of Hijrah (in 1984)

November

Fixed festivals

2nd   All Souls' Day
5th   Guy Fawkes Night
7th   U.S.S.R. National Day
11th   Remembrance Day
11th   Veterans' Day
30th   St Andrew's Day

Movable festivals
Guru Nanak's Birthday
Martyrdom of Guru Tegh Bahadur
Time of Sending Winter Clothes to Ancestors
Advent
Meelad-Ul-Nabi (in 1984, 1985, 1986)
Thanksgiving

December

Fixed festivals

16th   Day of the Covenant
21st   Forefathers' Day
25th   Christmas Day

Movable festivals
Enlightenment of the Buddha
Birthday of Guru Gobind Singh
Chanukah

Glossary

autumn The season of the year between summer and winter, falling between September and December in the northern hemisphere and between March and June in the southern hemisphere.

Buddha 'The Enlightened One', the name given to Prince Gautama who founded the religion of Buddhism in the sixth century B.C.

Buddhist A follower of the religion founded by Buddha.

calendar A system of measuring the passing of the years, and the parts of years.

Christian A follower of the religion founded by Jesus Christ.

Gregorian Calendar A calendar introduced by Pope Gregory in 1583 now used in all Christian countries and (for official purposes) in most other countries.

gurdwara A Sikh church.

harvest The period of gathering crops, which usually takes place in autumn.

hemisphere A half of the globe. In the northern hemisphere (between the equator and the North Pole) midwinter is in December and spring begins in March or April. In the southern hemisphere (between the equator and the South Pole) mid-winter is in June and spring begins in September or October.

Hindu A follower of Hinduism, the ancient religion of India.

Jesus Christ The founder of the Christian religion in the first century A.D.

Jew A follower of the Jewish religion, descended from the Hebrews of Biblical times who lived in the country now called Israel.

lunar calendar A calendar based – not upon the time taken for the earth to encircle the sun (about 365 days) – but upon the time taken for the moon to encircle the earth (twelve times in about 354 days).

Muhammed The founder of the Muslim religion in the seventh century A.D.

mosque A Muslim church.

Muslim A follower of the religion founded by Muhammed.

New Year The opening day, or first few days, of a year. The date can vary according to which calendar is used. In the Gregorian Calendar the date is 1st January. In lunar or lunisolar calendars the date varies each year.

patron saint A saint who is regarded as the special guardian of a country or of a movement.

remembrance A period during which people gratefully remember those who are dead, especially soldiers who died in a war.

saint A person of exceptional holiness in life who is regarded by Christians as being entitled to veneration after death and to a special place in Heaven.

Sikh A follower of the Sikh religion, founded by Guru Nanak in the fifteenth century A.D.

spring The season of the year between winter and summer, falling between March and June in the northern hemisphere and between September and December in the southern hemisphere.

synagogue A Jewish church.

Index